Ra

(Nachmanides)

The Disputation at Barcelona

Translated and Annotated by

Rabbi Dr. Charles B. Chavel

Ph.B., M.A., LL.B., D.H.L., D.D.

Cover Design: J.Neuman

www.bnpublishing.com
info@bnpublishing.com

For information regarding special discounts for bulk purchases, please contact BN Publishing at sales@bnpublishing.com

Preface

One of the most important events in Ramban's life, as well as in the annals of European Jewry, was a public disputation involving the fundamentals of Judaism. Ramban, the leading Jewish savant of the generation, was forced to defend the Judaic faith in the debate, which was held in Barcelona. Such events were not unique in Medieval Europe — others were held at various times — but the innovation which distinguishes this particular confrontation was that the State, in the person of King Jaime (or James) I of Aragonia, fully supported the venture. Moreover, not only did the monarch attend each session but he also joined in the discussion and personally delivered a final address to the assembled Jews in the synagogue urging them to abandon their faith.

The disputation was actually held in four separate sessions. The first was on Friday, July 20, 1263 (Ramban's account of this initial meeting is set forth in Paragraphs 2-35). The second was on Monday July 23 (Paragraphs 36-71), the third on Thursday, July 26 (Paragraphs 72-78), and the fourth on Friday, July 27 (Paragraphs 79-100).[1] Except

(1) The corresponding dates in the Jewish calendar are: Friday, Ab 12, Monday, Ab 15, Thursday, Ab 18, and Friday, Ab 19, 5023 (based on A.A. Akavia, "Calendar for 6,000 Years," Mosad Harav Kook, Jerusalem).

Note that references in the footnotes to other discourses refer to Ramban's Writings & Discourses. Other quotations of Ramban refer to the Commentary on the Torah, translated by Dr. Charles B. Chavel, published by Shilo Publishing House, Inc.

for the second session which took place in a monastery, all sessions were held at the royal palace. Ramban indicates that the meetings were well attended by various dignitaries of Church and State and by Jews of the local community. Besides the four formal sessions, there was an additional encounter on Saturday, August 4, the second Sabbath[2] after the final session. It occurred in the synagogue in the presence of the entire Jewish community (see Paragraphs 102-108).

Fortunately, Ramban preserved a faithful account of what transpired at all of these confrontations by recording them in Hebrew. There is a much briefer Latin protocol which offers the Church's version of the event, but glaringly absent in the protocol are Ramban's salient points with which he utterly refutes all the arguments of his apostate opponent, Pablo Christiani (or Fray Pul, as Ramban calls him) and makes him appear as a mere ignorant affront to the intelligence.

In the various introductions to Ramban's other works we have already touched upon the ramifications of the disputation on Ramban's life. We have mentioned the reason why in his old age, he had to abandon his home in Spain as a result of the disputation and how he chose to spend his final years in the Land of Israel. The disputation, however, was highly significant in itself, as is evident from these points:

All sources indicate that Ramban stood alone to discuss and defend his faith in the Catalonian language—and probably parts thereof even in Latin—in the face of an audience which was comprised of the foremost dignitaries in the kingdom of Aragonia. This in itself reveals much about the nature of his personality, that he knew how to comport himself in dignity in the presence of those dignitaries.

At various points throughout the debate, King Jaime manifests a sense of true respect and profound admiration for Ramban. The royal gift given Ramban when the sessions were completed eloquently attests to this.

(2) This was on the Sabbath, Ab 26, *Parshath R'eih*.

There can be absolutely no doubt of the utter veracity of Ramban's account. Knowing how carefully his enemies watched his every move, he would not have risked his life by writing anything untrue, especially since he well knew that the account would eventually reach the attention of the king.

Finally, at the end of this tortuous road, when iniquity was being silenced, we can feel Ramban's unuttered paean of thanksgiving for not having failed the challenge. This is reminiscent of David of old, who, when faced by Goliath and surrounded by the Philistine enemies, declared to the giant warrior, *Thou comest to me with a sword, and with a spear, and with a javelin, but I come to thee in the name of the Eternal of hosts . . . that all the earth may know that there is a G-d in Israel* (I Samuel 17:45-46).[3]

The translation of this work is based upon the Steinschneider Hebrew text as printed in the Kithvei Haramban, Vol. I, pp. 302-320. It should be stressed that this translation was not made for the purpose of any controversy or confrontation. Because it was written by Ramban, it is Torah, and bears its message for all times, and in that spirit it is presented here.

(3) Rabbi Yaakov Emden, the great fearless eighteenth century critic, speaks of Ramban in most laudatory terms. He alludes to Ramban's role in the disputation as "having stretched out his hand into the reptile's den" and coming out unharmed. See Abraham Bik's "Zoharei Yavetz," Introduction, p. 24.

THE DISPUTATION AT BARCELONA

BY OUR MASTER

RABBI MOSHE THE SON OF NACHMAN

THE GERONDITE

The Disputation at Barcelona

1 We have learned in [Tractate] Sanhedrin: [1] "The Rabbis taught [in a Beraitha]: [2] The Nazarene had five disciples: Matai,[3] Nakai,[4] Neitzer,[4] Bunai,[5] and Todah. They [the officers of the court] brought up Matai, and he said to them, 'Shall Matai be put to death? Is it not written. *'Mathai' (When) shall I come and appear before G-d?'* [6] However, they said to him, 'Yes, Matai shall be slain, for it is written, *'Mathai' (When) shall he die, and his name perish?'* [7] They brought up Nakai, and he said to them, 'Shall Nakai be put to death? Is it not written, *'V'naki' (And the innocent) and righteous slay thou not?'* [8] However, they said to him, 'Yes, Nakai shall be slain, for it is written, *In secret places, he slays 'naki' (the innocent).'* [9] They brought up Neitzer, and he said to them, 'Shall Neitzer be put to death? Is it not written, *'V'neitzer' (And a twig) shall grow forth out of his roots?'* [10] However, they said to him, 'Yes, Neitzer shall be slain, for it is written,

(1) Sanhedrin 43b. This passage was omitted from our editions by the censors, but it is found in earlier manuscripts. (2) It should be noted that the Hebrew text of the Disputation printed by Moshe Steinschneider confuses the verses quoted by the speakers in this first paragraph. In our English translation, we have followed the correct version as it appears in Omissions of the Talmud and as quoted correctly in Menorath Hama'or, Mosad Harav Kook, p. 165. (3) Matthew. (4) Lukas, or Luke. See Jastrow under the name Nakai. See *ibid.*, also for the following name, Neitzer. (5) Or Buni (*ibid.*) (6) Psalms 42:3. (7) *Ibid.*, 41:6. (8) Exodus 23:7. (9) Psalms 10:8. (10) Isaiah 11:1.

But thou art cast forth away from thy grave 'k'neitzer' (like an) abhorred (offshoot).' [11] They brought up Bunai, and he said to them, 'Shall Bunai be slain? Is it not written, *'B'ni' (My son) My firstborn is Israel?'* [12] However, they said to him, 'Yes, Bunai shall be slain, for it is written, *Behold, I will slay bincha' (thy son), thy firstborn.'* [13] They brought up Todah, and he said to them, 'Shall Todah be slain? Is it not written, *A psalm 'l'thodah' (of thanksgiving)*?' [14] However, they said to him, 'Yes, Todah shall be slain, for it is written, *Whoso offereth the sacrifice of 'todah' (thanksgiving) honoreth Me.'* '" [15] Rabbi Shlomo [Rashi] commented: "They [the five people mentioned] were influential with the [Roman] government, and it was [therefore] necessary to disprove all their futile arguments [for clemency]." In line with this thought, I am recording what I retorted to the mocking of Fray Pul, who publicly disgraced his education[16] in the presence of our lord the king—may his splendor be enhanced and his kingdom be exalted—and his scholars and counsellors.

2 Our lord the king commanded me to discuss with Fray Pul in his [and his counsellors'] presence in his [royal] palace in Barcelona. I replied saying, "I shall do according to the command of my lord the king [only] if you will permit me to speak freely, and for this I desire the permission of the king and the leave of Fray Ramon de Penyafort[17] and his colleagues who are here."

3 Fray Ramon (de Penyafort) answered, "[Permission is granted] with the proviso that you do not say anything objectionable [to our faith]."

(11) *Ibid.*, 14:19. (12) Exodus 4:22. (13) *Ibid.*, Verse 23. (14) Psalms 100:1. (15) *Ibid.*, 50:23. (16) Berachoth 17b. This expression is a euphemism for the apostate who misapplies his learning and disgraces his faith. (17) Fray Ramon, head of the Dominican Order and a leading figure in the activities of the Church in Barcelona, played a major role in the disputation proceedings. See Paragraphs 15-18 and 82.

4 I said to them, "I do not wish to enter with you into a discussion about this [entire matter]. However, in the course of the disputation, I must be free to speak [my mind] just as you are free to speak whatever you wish. [Of course], I have [sufficient] knowledge of good taste [so that I will] not overstep the bounds thereof, but I must have freedom of speech." They all gave me leave to speak freely.

5 Thus, I began by saying, "[Previous] disputations between gentiles[18] and Jews concerned many facets of religious observances upon which the fundamental principle of faith is not dependent. However, in this royal court, I wish to debate only about matters upon which the entire controversy is contingent."

6 They all replied, saying, "You have spoken well." Thus, we agreed to speak first on the subject of the Messiah, [that is], whether he had already come, which is the belief of the Christians, or was still to come, which is the belief of the Jews. Afterwards, we would discuss whether the Messiah is really G-d or is really mortal, born of a man and a woman. We would then discuss that the Jews hold the true Torah, or whether the Christians fulfill it.

7 Fray Pul commenced by asserting that he would prove from our Talmud that the Messiah, whom the prophets foretold, had already come.

8 I retorted, "Before we debate on this [point], I wish that he would teach me and inform me how it is possible [to prove his assertion from the Talmud]. I have heard that while Fray [Pul] traveled in Provence and many [other] places, he made a similar statement to many Jews, at which I am very much amazed. He should tell me [now] whether he intends to state that the Sages of the Talmud believed that the Nazarene was the Messiah and that they further believed that he was

(18) In Eisenstein's version: "priests."

[both] an actual [mortal] man and a true deity, which is the opinion of the Christians. Indeed, is it not known that the affair of the Nazarene took place in [the era of] the Second Temple and that he was born and killed before the destruction of the Temple? The Sages of the Talmud, such as Rabbi Akiba and his colleagues, lived after the destruction, and those who taught the Mishnah—Rabbi [Yehudah Hanasi] and Rabbi Nathan[19]—lived many years after the destruction. Rav Ashi, who compiled and edited the Talmud, certainly lived about four hundred years after the destruction.[20] If these Sages believed in the uniqueness of the Nazarene [and if they believed] that he is true and his belief and faith are true, then, if they wrote those things from which Fray Pul says that he will prove [his claim], how could they have remained in the Jewish religion and in their former way of life? They were Jews, they remained in the Jewish religion all their lives, and they died as Jews—they and their children and their disciples who heard all their teachings from their mouths! Why did they not apostatize and turn to the Nazarene's religion as did Fray Pul, who understood from their words that the faith of the Christians is the true religion—far be it!—and defected [from the Jewish faith] because of them? Rather, they and their disciples who received Torah from their mouths lived and died as Jews, such as we are today! It is they, [the Sages of the Talmud], who taught us the religion of Moses and Jewish custom. All of our deeds today are in accordance with the Talmud from the time it was composed until now, and with our observations of how the Sages of the Talmud were accustomed to doing things. The sole purpose of the entire Talmud is to teach us the customs of the Torah and the

(19) Baba Metzia 86a: "Rabbi [Yehudah Hanasi] and Rabbi Nathan [lived] at the end [of the era] of the Mishnah" [end of the first century, Common Era]. (20) The destruction of the Second Temple took place in the year 3828 after the Creation of the world, and Rav Ashi died in the year 4186 (Seder Hadoroth). The intervening lapse is thus only 358 years. Hence, Ramban approximates as "about four hundred years." Perhaps Ramban used the estimated figure because he took into consideration the fact that Rav Ashi himself did not complete the Talmud; his disciples finished it seventy-three years after his death.

commandment and how [our] ancestors conducted themselves in [the time of] the Temple according to the command of the prophets and that of Moses our teacher, peace be upon him. However, if they [truly] believed in the Nazarene and his religion, why did they not do as Fray Pul, who [apparently] understands their words better than they themselves did!"

9 Fray Pul replied, "These are long-winded words, [spoken] in order to evade [the issues of] the disputation. Nevertheless, you will listen to what I say."

10 I said to [the king and his counsellors], "To me, this is a clear indication that he will not be saying things of substance, but I will [submit to] hear them because it is the will of my lord the king."

11 [Fray Pul] then began, "Behold, Scripture states, *The sceptre shall not depart from Judah,* etc., *until 'Shiloh' cometh.*[21] [The word *Shiloh*] refers to the Messiah. The prophet [Jacob] is thus saying that Judah will always retain power until the Messiah will come from him. If so, since you have neither one tribe nor a ruler's staff today, the Messiah who is of his descendants and who has the rulership must have already come."

12 I replied, "The purport of the prophet [Jacob] is not to state that the kingdom of Judah will never be devoid of power at any time [until the advent of the Messiah]. Rather, he is saying that [power] will never be removed or depart from him completely. The intent thereof is that as long as kingship continues in Israel, it belongs to Judah. If their kingdom will be [temporarily] discontinued because of sin, [the kingship] will return to [the tribe of] Judah [when it will ultimately be restored].[22] The proof for my words is that for many years, before the

(21) Genesis 49:10. (22) See Ramban's commentary on the verse, *ibid.*, Genesis, pp. 586-590, where this thought is developed at greater length.

Nazarene, Judah, not Israel had been divested of royalty,[23] and for many years, monarchy ceased both in Israel and in Judah, because in the seventy years during which [the Jews] were exiled to Babylon, there was no royalty whatsoever in either Judah or Israel. During [the era of] the Second Temple, there was no king over Judah except for Zerubbabel and his sons,[24] who ruled only a short period of time. The people then remained [without a king] for 380 years,[25] during which time the priests of the House of the Hasmoneans and their servants [the Herodians] ruled, until the destruction [of the Second Temple]. Certainly, now, when the people are in exile, [they have no ruler from Judah], for if there is no people [with their own homeland], there is no king."

13 Fray Pul answered, "Although the Jews had no kings during all those times, they nevertheless had men of authority [who were descendants of the House of David]. Thus did they interpret in the Talmud: [26] '*The sheivet (sceptre) shall not depart from Judah.*[21] This alludes to the Exilarchs in Babylon, who ruled the people with the *sheivet* (rod). [The verse continues], *nor the ruler's staff from between his feet.*[21] This alludes to the descendants of Hillel who teach Torah in public [in the Land of Israel].' Today, however, you have no such ordination as it was known in [the era of] the Talmud, and that authority [of the Exilarchs] has ceased. Today, therefore, no one has the right to call himself 'Rabbi.' Their calling you '*Maestro*' (Master) is a mistake, and you are using that title falsely."

(23) The Herodians who ruled Israel towards the end of the Second Temple era were not of the tribe of Judah. (24) Zerubbabel was succeded by his son Meshullam (Seder Olam Zuta), who was followed by his son Chananyah (Yochasin). (25) The period of Grecian domination lasted 180 years, the Hasmonean kingdom 103, the Herodian kingdom 103, (Abodah Zarah 9a), a total of 386 years. Meshullam son of Zerubbabel died at the beginning of the rule of Alexander the Great, who initiated the era of Grecian domination. The figure of 380 mentioned by Ramban is thus approximate. (26) Sanhedrin 5a.

14 I answered scoffingly, "This matter is not among [those agreed upon for] disputation. Nevertheless, you are not saying the truth. 'Rabbi' is not the rendition of *'Maestro;'* 'Rav' is identical with *'Maestro,'* and in the Talmud, [scholars] are called 'Rav' [even] without ordination.[27] However, I will agree that I am neither a Master nor even a proficient scholar." I said this [last] by way of good taste, and I returned [to the matter at hand by] saying to him, "I will inform you that our Rabbis of blessed memory intended to explain the verse, [*The sceptre shall not depart from Judah,* etc.], only with regard to real kingship. However, you do not understand law and statute except for the few homilies with which you have accustomed yourself. What the Sages mentioned [about the Exilarchs in Babylon, etc.], is based on the following consideration: According to strict law, a single judge [in a case] is exempt from paying [for an incorrect decision he rendered] only if he received permission [to dispense justice] from the *Nasi* (Prince) who is identical with the king. The Rabbis further stated that in the time of the exile, since there are some royal descendants [of the House of David], they who are authorized by the rulers of the nations [to dispense justice]—such as the Exilarchs of Babylon and the Princes of the Land of Israel—have the right to grant [others] permission [to exercise judicial authority] and ordination. This practice continued among the Sages of the Talmud for more than four hundred years after the Nazarene.[28] The opinion of the Sages of the Talmud is not

(27) In the Land of Israel, ordination—the process of investiture with judicial rights and functions—was conferred by three Sages, of whom only one had to be duly ordained. The authority bestowed by ordination in the Land of Israel was also effective outside of the Land of Israel. Ordination was conferred until about the end of the fourth century, Common Era, when the academies in the Land of Israel dwindled, on account of the Roman persecution, and the Babylonian Talmud was compiled there about a century later. A careful reading of the Talmud reveals this distinction: the Masters who were ordained in the Land of Israel are called "Rabbi" [like Rabbi Yochanan] while the Babylonian Masters were called "Rav" [like Rav Yehudah]. (28) The Nazarene was born close to the year 3671, about two hundred years before the destruction of the Second Temple in the year 3828 (see Paragraph

that there will always be a *sceptre* or *ruler's staff* which will belong to Judah. Rather, the prophet [Jacob] promised Judah that Jewish kingship will be his, and he assured him [only] concerning actual kingship. Nevertheless, it ceased for many years as I have mentioned. During the time of the Babylonian exile, neither *a sceptre* nor *a ruler's staff* was among them at all, and during [the era of] the Second Temple when kingship was held by the [Hasmonean] priests and their [Herodian] servants, the tribe of Judah had no authority either as Exilarch or as *Nasi* because leadership and authority belonged to the kings who were priests, to their judges and officers, and to those who found favor in their eyes."

15 Fray Pere of Genoa[29] then answered, "This is true. Scripture states only that [the sceptre] shall not cease completely, but there can be a temporary cessation, [which is called] *vagare* in the [Latin] vernacular."

16 I remarked to the king, "You see, Fray Pere agrees with me."

17 Fray Pere said, "I did not [actually] agree. Seventy years of the Babylonian [exile] is but a brief period of time, and many [of the people who returned from Babylon to build the Second Temple] remembered the First Temple, as is written in the Book of Ezra.[30] This [type of lapse] is called 'cessation' or *vagare,* in the vernacular.

22). "In the year 4119 (359 Common Era), in the days of Hillel, son of Rabbi Yehudah Nesiah, the Sanhedrin ceased in the Land of Israel" (Ramban in Sefer Hazakith on Tractate Gittin, Chapter 4). Thus, from 3671, the approximate year of the Nazarene's birth, until the year 4119, when the Sanhedrin ceased, there are 448 years. When we substract the years of the Nazarene's life from this figure, we can see why Ramban states here that the practice of judicial authority existed "more than four hundred years after the Nazarene." See in *Sefer Hakabalah* (The Book of Tradition) by Abraham ibn David, on the date of the Nazarene's birth. (29) He was head of the Franciscan Order. (30) Ezra 3:12.

However, now that [the exile] has endured for a thousand years and more, the removal [of the sceptre] is [obviously] complete."

18 I replied, "Now you are changing your mind. [The term] 'removal' applies to a thing which will come back. In the words of the prophet, there is no differentiation between [an interruption of] many years and [one] or [just] a few years. Besides, the times I mentioned, [i.e., the years throughout the entire Second Temple era during which Judah did not possess kingship], constitute a long period. Moreover, our patriarch Jacob of blessed memory did not promise Judah that the *sceptre* and *ruler's staff* will be his only over his own tribe. Instead he gave him kingship over all Israel, as it is written, *Judah, thee shall thy brethren praise.*[31] It is further written, *For Judah prevailed above his brethren, and of him came he that is the prince.*[32] Yet, from the death of [King] Solomon, [at which time Jeroboam founded the kingdom of Israel, which consisted of ten of the twelve tribes], Judah's royal rule ceased over these tribes, as it is written, *There was none that followed the House of David, but the tribe of Judah only.*[33] Thus, it can be clearly concluded that the prophet [Jacob] said only that kingship will not be removed completely. The truth is that during the time of exile, [lack of kingship in the tribe of Judah] cannot be termed 'a removal' or 'a cessation' at all. [It is only a 'temporary cessation'], for [the lack of authority] is not because of Judah; [it is due], rather, to the part of the people. The prophet did not promise Judah that Israel would never go into exile so that he could rule over them [in their own land] at all times."

19 Fray Pul then reverted [to the original topic], arguing that they say in the Talmud that the Messiah had already come. He quoted the homily in the Midrash on Lamentations[34] concerning a [Jewish]

(31) Genesis 49:8. (32) I Chronicles 5:2. (33) I Kings 12:20. The tribe of Benjamin is included in that of Judah, as Jerusalem belonged to both (R'dak). (34) Eichah Rabbathi 1:51, with minor changes.

ploughman whose cow lowed while he was ploughing. A passing Arab called to him, "Israelite, Israelite, untie thy cow, untie thy plough, take apart thy ploughshare, for the Temple has been destroyed." So he untied the cow, untied the plough and disassembled the ploughshare. The cow then lowed a second time. The Arab said to him, "Tie thy cow, tie thy plow, tie thy ploughshare, for your Messiah has been born."

20 I responded, "I am not receptive to this homily, but it is a proof to my words."

21 [Fray Pul] shouted, "See, he [himself] is renouncing their [sacred] books!"

22 I elaborated, "Truly, I do not believe that Messiah was born on the day of the [Temple's] destruction. Either this homily is not true or it has another meaning, [which lies] among the secrets of the Sages. Yet, [even if] I would accept its literal meaning as you have expressed it, then it is a proof for my contention, for this [Midrash] relates that the Messiah was born on the day of the destruction, after that event. If so, the Nazarene could not be the Messiah as you have said, for he was born and was killed before the destruction. According to the truth, his birth took place about two hundred years before the destruction,[28] and according to your reckoning, [it occurred] seventy-three years [before the destruction]." The man was thereupon silenced.

23 Master Guillem, one of the royal judges, commented, "The present discussion is not about the Nazarene, but whether the Messiah had come or not. You have stated that he has not come, but this book of yours says that he did come."

24 I replied to him, "You chose to answer with typical legal deceit. Nevertheless, I will answer you concerning this. The Sages did not say that [the Messiah] had come; they said that he was born [on the day of

the destruction]. Moses our teacher did not come [before Pharaoh] on the day he was born, nor was he a redeemer at that time. However, when he came before Pharaoh by command of the Holy One, blessed be He, and said to him, *Thus saith the Eternal, the G-d of Israel: Let My people go,* etc.,[35] then [it could be said that] he had come. Similarly, when the Messiah will come to the Pope and say to him by the command of G-d, 'Let My people go,' [it will be said of him that] he has come. To this day, however, he has not yet come, nor is he the Messiah at all. When King David was born, he was neither king nor the anointed one, but when Samuel anointed him, then he became the anointed one [i.e., the king]. On the day when Elijah [the prophet] will anoint [the true redeemer] as a Messiah by command of G-d, then he will [correctly] be called 'Messiah.' Afterwards, when he will come to the Pope in order to redeem us, then it will be said that the redeemer has come."

25 [Master Guillem] argued, "There is the section [beginning with the verse], *Behold, My servant shall prosper,*[36] which narrates the matter of the death of the Messiah and how he fell into the hands of the wicked, as it was with the Nazarene. [Do] you believe that this chapter deals with the Messiah?"

26 I said to him, "According to its true sense, it speaks only generally of the people of Israel, for the prophets always call him *Israel, My servant,*[37] *O Jacob, My servant.*"[38]

27 Fray Pul said, "I see from the words of your Sages that [the section] speaks of the Messiah."

28 I replied to him, "It is true that in the books of Hagadoth (homilies), our Rabbis of blessed memory interpret [the passage] in

(35) Exodus 5:1. (36) Isaiah 52:13. (37) *Ibid.*, 41:8. (38) *Ibid.*, 44:1.

connection with the Messiah, but they have never said that he will be killed by his enemies. You will never find in any book of Jewish tradition—neither the Talmud nor the Hagadoth—that the Messiah son of David will be killed, that he will be handed over into the hands of his enemies, or that he will be buried with the wicked. Your alleged deliverer was not even buried, [and so does not fulfill the requirements of your interpretation]. I will clearly and well explain to you the passage [*Behold, My servant shall prosper*],[36] and [that section, as you will hear], contains no reference to the fact that he will be killed, as your deliverer was." They, however, did not want to hear [my explanation].

29 [Fray Pul] reverted [to the original theme] and said that it is explained in the Talmud[39] that Rabbi Yehoshua ben Levi asked Elijah [the prophet], "When will Messiah come?" He answered him, "Ask Messiah himself." He said, "Where is he?" [Elijah] replied, "At the gate of Rome, among the sick." So [Rabbi Yehoshua ben Levi] went there, and he found him. He asked him, etc.[40] Thus, he had already come, and he is the Nazarene, who rules in Rome.

30 I retorted, "Is it not clearly written here that he has not come? Did [the Rabbi] not ask Elijah, 'When *will* he come?' Similarly, [the Rabbi] asked the Messiah, 'When *will* the master come?' Thus, he had not yet come although according to the literal meaning of these homilies, he was already born, but I do not believe[41] in that."

31 Our lord king then asked, "If [the Messiah] was born on the day of the destruction of the Temple, which occurred more than a

(39) Sanhedrin 98a. (40) He asked him when he will come. The Messiah replied, "Today." When the day passed and he did not come, the Rabbi complained to Elijah. Elijah answered that the Messiah was referring to the verse, *Today, if ye would but hearken to His voice* (Psalms 95:7). In other words, he is prepared to come today, if we will hearken to G-d's voice. (41) See further in Paragraph 39, and Note 46.

thousand years ago,[42] and he has not come yet, how can he [possibly] come [anymore]? It is not in man's nature to live a thousand years!"

32 I answered him, "One of the conditions we have already made is that I would not dispute with you and that you would not participate in the arguments. However, [in response to your question], among the ancients there have already been [men such as] Adam and Methuselah,[43] who lived close to a thousand years. Elijah and Enoch lived [even] longer, for life is from G-d."

33 He said, "And where is he today?"

34 I answered, "That is not pertinent to the discussion, and I will not answer you. Perhaps you will find him at the gates of Toledo if you will send one of your royal messengers posthaste." I said that [last remark] mockingly.

35 At that point, they arose, and the king set the time to resume the debate on the following Monday.

36 On that day, the king went to one of the cloisters in the city, and all the people of the city, gentiles and Jews, were gathered there. Among them were the bishop [of Barcelona] and all the priests, Franciscan scholars, and preachers. [Fray Pul] arose to speak.

37 I said to our lord the king, "My lord, hear me [first]." Despite [my request], he said to me, "He should speak first, for he is the claimant."

(42) The destruction occurred in the year 3828, and this disputation was held in 5023. The difference between them is thus 1,195, "more than a thousand years." (43) Adam lived 930 years (Genesis 5:5), while Methuselah lived 969 years (*ibid.*, Verse 27). Elijah ascended to heaven alive (II Kings 2:11), and so did Enoch (Genesis 5:24).

38 I persisted, "Let me explain my opinion about the Messiah, and then he[44] will be able to answer clearly."

39 I then arose and stated, "*Hear, ye peoples, all of you.*[45] Fray Pul asked me whether the Messiah, of whom the prophets spoke, had already come, and I said that he had not come. He then brought a book of Agadah (homilies) in which it is stated that the Messiah was born on the day the Temple was destroyed. I said, even though, that I do not believe in this, that passage would support my words. I shall now explain to you why I said that I do not believe in this [passage]. You should know that we have three kinds of books. The first is the Bible, and all of us believe in it in perfect faith. The second is what is called the Talmud, which is the commentary on the commandments of the Torah. There are 613 Commandments in the Torah, and there is not one of them which is not explained in the Talmud. We [firmly] believe in [the Talmud's] explanations of the commandments. We have a third book called Midrash, meaning sermons. It is just as if the bishop would rise and deliver a sermon, and one of the listeners whom the sermon pleased recorded it. With regard to this book [of sermons], if one believes in it, it is well and good; if one does not believe in it, he will not be harmed [spiritually]. We have Sages who wrote that the Messiah will not be born until the time near the end [of the exile], at which time he will come to redeem us from the exile. Therefore, I do not believe the statement of this book that he was born on the day of the destruction. We also call [the Midrash] the book of Hagadah, meaning *Razionamiento*. That is to say, it is nothing more than matters which one person tells another.[46] However, I do accept this

(44) Another version: "I would be able to answer clearly on the rest of his words." (45) Micah 1:2. (46) It should be pointed out that certain Agadoth (homilies) of the Midrash are expressed in a recondite language, with undoubtedly some hidden meaning contained therein (see Paragraph 22). Ramban, however, confronted as he was by the apostate, and in order to quelch any further questioning into the hidden meaning of the Agadah, answered him as stated. See further on this point in the notes on the Disputation in Kithvei Haramban, Vol. I, pp. 308-309.

homily in its literal sense as you would have it. It is a clear proof that your Nazarene is not the Messiah that you claim for yourselves, for he was not born on that day [of the destruction of the Temple. In fact], long before that time, the whole affair [of his life] had already passed. You, our lord king, have wondered and raised a better objection than they. [You have objected] that it is not in the nature of man to live a thousand years. I will now provide a clear answer to your question. Behold, the first man lived 930 years.[47] Scripture explains that he died because of his sin[48] and that had he not sinned, he would have lived many more [years] or [perhaps] forever. All of us, gentiles and Jews, admit that the sin and punishment of the first man will be voided in the era of the Messiah.[49] If so, death will cease from all of us [ordinary mortals] after the coming of Messiah. As far as the Messiah himself is concerned, death is completely inoperative against him. Thus, it is fitting that Messiah live for thousands of years or [even] forever. Accordingly, the psalm states, *He asked life of Thee, Thou gavest it him, [even length of days forever and ever].*[50] This [matter] has [now] been elucidated.

40 "Our lord king, you have further asked, Where he [the Messiah] stays. The answer is clearly written in Scripture. The first man was placed in the Garden of Eden, which is upon the earth. When he sinned, it is stated, *And the Eternal G-d sent him forth from the Garden of Eden.*[51] If so, this one, who is free from the punishment of man, abides there in the Garden of Eden. The Sages so stated in the book of Hagadoth (homilies) which I have mentioned."

41 The king said, "Have you not stated in that Hagadah that he is in Rome?"

(47) Genesis 5:5. (48) *Ibid.,* 2:17 and 3:19. (49) Shemoth Rabbah 30:2: "In the days of the Messiah, the Holy One, blessed be He, will cause death to be swallowed up." (50) Psalms 21:5. (51) Genesis 3:23.

42 I answered him, "I did not say that he is permanently stationed in Rome but that he was seen in Rome on a certain day. Elijah told that Sage [Rabbi Yehoshua ben Levi] that he will find him there on that day, and he was [indeed] seen there. His appearance there was for the reason mentioned in the homilies, which I do not want to declare before so many people." This was because I did not want to tell them that in the Hagadah,[52] it is stated that the Messiah will remain in Rome until he will destroy it. This is similar to what we find in the case of Moses our teacher. He was raised in the house of Pharaoh [himself] until [the latter] received his punishment from Moses, who drowned all of [Pharaoh's] people in the sea. It is also as stated [in the case] of King Hiram of Tyre, *Therefore have I brought forth a fire from the midst of thee, it hath devoured thee.*[53] Thus, Isaiah stated, *There shall the calf feed, and there shall he lie down, and consume the branches thereof.*[54] In Pirkei Heichaloth,[55] it states [that the destruction of Rome will be pervasive and thorough] "to the extent that one man will say to the other, 'Here is Rome and everything in it for a *p'rutah* (the smallest coin),' and he will answer him, 'I do not want it.' " I privately communicated all this to the king.

43 I [further] challenged, "Do you agree with my words that the sin of Adam will be nullified in the time of the Messiah?"

44 Our lord king and Fray Pul rejoined, "Yes, [we do agree], but not as you think. Actually, all [generations] enter Gehenna because of that punishable act. In the days of the Nazarene, the deliverer, [the penalty] was removed, for he freed them from there."

45 I replied, "In our country, they say that he who wishes to tell a lie has his witnesses live far away. There are many punishments written

(52) I do not know the source of the Hagadah referred to here. (53) Ezekiel 28:18. (54) Isaiah 27:10. (55) Pirkei Heichaloth 6:2, in Wertheimer's Bathei Midrashoth, Vol. I, p. 75.

[in Scripture] with reference to Adam and Eve: *Cursed is the ground for thy sake;*[56] *Thorns and thistles shall it bring forth to thee;*[57] *In the sweat of thy face [shall thou eat bread]; for dust thou art, [and unto dust shalt thou return].*[58] Similarly, with regard to the woman, it states, *In pain thou shalt bring forth children.*[59] All of these [punishments] are still in effect today. Thus, all [punishments] that are observable and perceivable have not been atoned for in the era of your deliverer but you assert that the [affliction of] Gehenna, which is not [among the punishments] enumerated there [in Scripture], is forgiven. [You make this assertion] because there is no one to contradict you. *Send one of you,*[60] and let him come and tell [us whether Gehenna still exists or not]. Moreover, *Far be it from G-d, [that He should do wickedness].*[61] The righteous are not doomed [to suffer] the punishment of Gehenna because of the sin of the first man, their ancestor. My soul has the same identical affinity to the soul of my father as it does to that of Pharaoh, but my soul will not enter Gehenna because of Pharaoh's sin! The punishments [for the first man's sin] relate only to the body, because my body comes from my father and my mother. When [eventual death] was decreed for both [Adam and Eve] and they became mortal, all their descendants became subject to mortality in a natural way."

46 [Fray Pul] then stood up and declared, "I will bring further proof that the time for [the advent of] the Messiah has passed."

47 I said, "My lord king, bear with me [a while]. The essence of our judgment, truth, and statute does not depend upon the Messiah. [For the purpose of fulfilling the commandments of the Torah], you are more beneficial to me than the Messiah. You are king, and he is king. You are a gentile king, and he is a Jewish king, for the Messiah is but a

(56) Genesis 3:17. (57) *Ibid.*, Verse 18. (58) *Ibid.*, Verse 19. (59) *Ibid.*, Verse 16. (60) *Ibid.*, Verse 42:16. (61) Job 34:10.

king of flesh and blood like you. When I worship my Creator in your dominion, exiled [from my homeland] suffering and under subjugation, *the shame of the nations*[62] who taunt me always,[63] my reward is abundant, for I bring a whole-offering to G-d from my physical being. Because of that, I shall increasingly merit life in the World to Come. However, when a king of Israel, [a monarch] of my faith, will rule over all the nations and I will have no choice but to abide by the law of the Jews, my reward will not be as abundant. Nevertheless, the vital conflict and difference between the Jews and the Christians concerns your contention about the principle of G-d, [a suggestion] which is extremely unpalatable to the mind. All of your life, you, our lord king, a Christian son of a Christian father and mother, have heard priests, monks, and preachers speaking of the Nazarene's birth. They have filled your mind and the marrow of your bones with this thing, and it comes to you [now] out of habit. Yet, what you believe—and it is the root of your faith—is not acceptable to the [rational] mind. Nature does not work that way, and the prophets never said so. Furthermore, a miracle cannot disseminate itself in that way, as I shall explain[64] with valid proofs in its place and in its time. The mind of any Jew or any man will not permit him to believe that the Creator of heaven and earth [and all that is therein] would pass through the womb of a Jewish woman, to develop there for seven months,[65] [at which point] an infant was born, [who supposedly is G-d] and who afterwards grew up and later was turned over into the hands of his enemies, who judged him, condemned him to death, and killed him. You then claim, finally, that he became alive and returned to his former state [of divinity]! You voice your opinion in vain and to no

(62) Ezekiel 36:16. See in "The Book of Redemption," end of the Second Gate, where Ramban restates the same thought. (63) See Psalms 102:9. (64) Ramban must be referring to the preceding clause, "and the prophets never said so," which is fully explained in his commentary on the Scriptural passage which commences with, *Behold, My servant shall prosper*. See Kithvei Haramban, Vol. I, pp. 322-326. (65) Another version: "for nine months."

purpose, for this is the root of the controversy between us! Nevertheless, we shall also speak about the Messiah [an issue secondary to the principal point of contention, as I explained], in accordance with your wish.

48 Fray Pul inquired, "Do you [yourself] believe that he has already come?"

49 I answered, "No, I believe and know, rather, that he has not come. Besides the Nazarene, there has never been a person in the world who himself said or of whom it was said that he is Messiah. It is impossible for me to accept that he is the Messiah, for the prophet has said of the Messiah, *He will have dominion from sea to sea, and from the river unto the ends of the earth.*[66] The Nazarene though, had no dominion. During his life, he was persecuted by his enemies and was in hiding from them. In the end, he fell into their hands and was not [even] able to help himself. How [then] could he help Israel? Even after his death, he had no dominion, for the might of Rome was not due to him. On the contrary, before [the Romans] believed in him, the city of Rome ruled over the greatest part of the world, but after they adopted his religion, they lost many kingdoms. At present, the worshippers of Mohammed have more [dominion and] power than [the Christians]. Similarly, the prophet states that in the time of the Messiah, *They shall teach no more every man his neighbor, and every man his brother, saying: Know the Eternal, for they shall all know Me,* etc.[67] It is further stated, *For the earth shall be full of the knowledge of the Eternal, as the waters cover the sea,*[68] and it is also said, *And they shall beat their swords into ploughshares, and their spears into pruning-hooks; nation shall not lift up sword against nation, neither shall they learn war any more.*[69] From the days of the

(66) Psalms 72:8. In other words, though the Nazarene was the only person until Ramban's time who ever claimed to be the Messiah, he never fulfilled the Messianic prophecies of the Scriptures, as Ramban continues. (67) Jeremiah 31:33. (68) Isaiah 11:9. (69) *Ibid.,* 2:4.

Nazarene until now, the entire world has been full of violence and robbery. [Indeed], the Christians spill more blood than the rest of the nations, and they also lead immoral lives. How difficult it would be for you, my lord king, and these your knights if they would *neither . . . learn war any more!* The prophet further said about the Messiah, *And he shall smite the land with the rod of his mouth.*[70] [The Rabbis] in the book of Hagadah which Fray Pul is holding explain it [as follows]: People will say to King Messiah, 'That country has rebelled against you.' He will declare, 'Let the locust come and lay it waste.' They will say to him, 'That district has rebelled against you.' He will say, 'Let [a horde of] mixed beasts come and destroy it.' This did not occur with the Nazarene. As for you, his servants, [despite your avowals of belief in the Nazarene's elimination of war], you [still] consider it advantageous to have [weapons and] mail-covered steeds. Yet, at times, *all this availeth nothing*[71] for you. I will yet bring you many proofs from the words of the prophets."

50 [Fray Pul] cried out, "It is his constant habit to deliver such long-winded speeches. Nevertheless, I have a question to ask."

51 The king instructed me: "Be silent. He is the one who is asking." Thus, I was silent.

52 [Fray Pul] said, "Your Sages say that the Messiah is honored above the angels, and this can only refer to the Nazarene, who is the deliverer and the deity." He brought proof from [the Rabbis'] statement in the Hagadah:[72] *"He shall be exalted and lifted up, and shall be very high.*[36] *He shall be exalted* above Abraham; *and lifted up* above Moses; *and shall be very high* above the ministering angels."

(70) *Ibid.*, 11:4. (71) Esther 5:13. In other words, even though you insist that the Nazarene has brought an end to evil, there is still suffering, war, and death pervading the world, and you are powerless before them. (72) Yalkuth Isaiah 476.

53 I explained to him, "Our Sages always say this about all the righteous: [73] 'The righteous are more distinguished than the ministering angels.' Moses our teacher also said to the angel,[74] 'In the place where I sit, you have no leave [even] to stand.'[75] Concerning Israel in general, they said: [76] 'Israel is beloved [by G-d] more than His ministering angels.' However, the intention of this master of the Hagadah concerning the Messiah is to state that our patriarch Abraham, peace be upon him, converted gentiles, preached the belief in the Creator, blessed be He, before the nations, and intrepidly differed with Nimrod, [the king of Babylon]. Moses, however, did a greater thing [than Abraham], for he stood humbly before Pharaoh, the great and wicked king, and did not curry his favor with the great plagues with which he smote him, and he took Israel out of his dominion. The ministering angels are extremely vigorous in the pursuit of the redemption [of Israel], as [the angel told Daniel], *And there is none that holdeth with me against thee, except Michael your prince.*[77] It is further said, *And now I will return to fight with the prince of Persia.*[78] The Messiah, though, will surpass them all, *and his heart will be lifted up in the ways of the Eternal.*[79] In the name of G-d, he will come and command the Pope and the kings of all the nations, *Let My people go, that they may serve Me,*[80] and he will perform many great signs and wonders and will not fear them at all. He will remain in their city of Rome until he will destroy it. If you desire, I will explain the entire passage [of *Behold, My servant shall prosper*]."[36] [Fray Pul], however, was unwilling.

54 He cited another Hagadah[81] which relates that the Messiah is praying that the Holy One, blessed be He, should forgive Israel their

(73) Sanhedrin 93a. (74) Sifre, *Nitzavim*, 308. (75) G-d had said to the angel of death, "Go, bring me the soul of Moses." Moses, however, said to the angel, "In the place where I sit, you have no leave to stand" (*ibid.*) (76) Chullin 91b. (77) Daniel 10:21. (78) *Ibid.*, Verse 20. (79) II Chronicles 17:6. (80) Exodus 8:16. (81) The source of this quotation is in the Midrash of Rabbi Moshe Hadarshan.

sins, and that he offered to accept suffering upon himself. However, he said before Him, "I accept suffering upon myself on the condition that the resurrection will occur in my time, [resurrection] not only for the dead of my generation alone, but for all the dead that have died from [the time of] the first man until now, and not only for those who died [a natural death], but also for those thrown into the sea who were drowned and those devoured by wolves and beasts." Now, [Fray Pul argued], the fate of suffering of the Messiah, is the slaying of the Nazarene, which he willingly accepted upon himself.

55 I responded, "Woe to the shameless one! The Nazarene did not do any of these. He did not resurrect the dead from [the time of] the first man until now or any of these [other] things. Besides, this prayer shows that [Messiah] is a mortal and not G-d, and he was not able to give life to the dead. However, these tribulations [which the Messiah undergoes, according to the Agadah],[72] are not [physical. They are] only the grief which he experiences because his coming is very greatly delayed. He sees his people in exile, *and there is nought in the power of* his *hand.*[82] He sees worshippers *of them that are no gods,*[83] and those who deny him and have made themselves another deliverer are more honored than his people."

56 [Fray Pul] reverted [to his questioning] and said, "Daniel stated, *Seventy weeks* [of years] *are decreed upon thy people and upon thy holy city, to finish the transgression, and to make an end of sin, and to forgive iniquity, and to bring in everlasting righteousness, and to seal vision and prophet, and to anoint the most holy one.*[84] The *seventy weeks* [of years] refer to [490] years, which are the 420 years of the existence of the Second Temple and the seventy years of the Babylonian exile. *The most holy one* is the Nazarene."

(82) Deuteronomy 28:32. (83) II Chronicles 13:9. (84) Daniel 9:24.—Since a week has seven days, *seventy weeks* would total 490 days, which in this verse, represent years. These correspond to the 490 years of the Babylonian exile and the era of the Second Temple, as explained in the text.

57 I retorted, "Did not the Nazarene [live] more than thirty *weeks* [of years or 210 years] before that time, according to our reckoning,[85] which is the truth that his contemporaries—those who knew him and recognized him—testified about him. Even according to your reckoning,[86] he [lived] more than ten *weeks* [or seventy years] before [the destruction]."

58 He argued, "Yes, it was so. However, in one verse it states, *Know therefore and discern, that from the going forth of the word to restore and to build Jerusalem unto one anointed, a prince.*[87] The *one anointed* is identical with the *prince,* who is the Nazarene."

59 I answered, "This, too, is an obvious error. Scripture divides the *seventy weeks* [of years][84] which [Daniel] mentioned, and [in the following verse], it enumerates from their [total]: *unto one anointed, a prince, shall be seven weeks* [of years].[87] Afterwards, [in the same verse], it mentions, *and for threescore and two weeks* [of years], *it shall be built again, with broad places and streets.*[87] Then it enumerates *one week, and half of the week,*[88] during which *he shall make a firm covenant with many.*[88] Thus *seventy weeks* [of years] are completed.[89] The Nazarene, whom you call the *anointed one, a*

(85) In Paragraph 22, Ramban states that "according to the truth, his [the Nazarene's] birth took place about two hundred years before the destruction." In the symbolic language of Daniel, a two hundred year period is approximately thirty *weeks* or 210 years. It should be noted, incidentally, that this chronology undermines the position of those enemies who taunt us that the Temple did not exist long after the Nazarene's death. A period of over a century and a half surely cannot be considered a short time. (86) According to their reckoning the Nazarene was born seventy-three years—more than ten *weeks*—before the destruction. See Paragraph 22. (87) Daniel 9:25. (88) *Ibid.,* Verse 27. (89) Seven *weeks* (*ibid.,* Verse 25) plus sixty-two (Verse 27) plus one and one-half equal seventy full weeks, which represent 490 years which elapsed from the beginning of the Babylonian exile to the destruction of the Second Temple, as mentioned above. Ramban will explain further that after seven *weeks* [or forty-nine years] of the Babylonian exile, Zerubbabel, prince of Judah, came to resettle the Land. The Temple, however, was not completed until seventy years had passed. See the Third Gate in Book of Redemption where these points are fully discussed and explained.

prince,[87] did not come after *seven weeks* [of years],[87] but after more than sixty weeks [of years] according to your reckoning.[86] If you would attempt to explain to me the entire chapter according to your line of thinking, I could refute you, for you will never be able to explain it [satisfactorily]. Yet, you shamelessly speak of a subject about which you know nothing. However, I shall inform you that the *anointed one, a prince,*[87] is Zerubbabel, who came at the time of *seven weeks* [of years],[87] for it is so explained in Scripture."

60 He objected, "But how could [Zerubbabel] be called the *anointed one?*"

61 I answered, "Cyrus, [king of Persia], is also [called] Messiah (the anointed one),[90] and regarding Abraham, Isaac, and Jacob, He said, *Touch not Mine anointed ones.*[91] It is said [of Zerubbabel] that he is a *nagid* (prince) in order to indicate that his dominion will not be uplifted, despite the fact that he was distinguished and honored among his people, as it is said, *The princes of the peoples are gathered together, the people of the G-d of Abraham.*[92] I am prepared to explain to you this entire chapter [in the Book of Daniel] if you and these your friends wish to learn and if you have the mind to understand. I declare before our lord king and all the peoples that the designated time for the coming of Messiah is not indicated in that chapter [quoted above] or in all the words of Daniel except for the end of [that] book. It is so explained in Scripture that with regard to what he was told in that chapter [mentioned above] and in other chapters, [Daniel] said that he was always praying that he might know 'the designated time.' Ultimately, they informed him of that 'designated time' in the verse which states, *And from the time that the continual burnt-offering shall be taken away, and the detestable thing that causeth appalment set up, there shall be a thousand two hundred and ninety days.*[93] In the presence of the peoples, I shall now explain the

(90) See Isaiah 45:1. (91) Psalms 105:15. (92) *Ibid.*, 47:10. (93) Daniel 12:11.

meaning of this verse although it may be hard upon the Jews who are here.[94] He is saying that from the time the burnt-offering will be taken away until 'the detestable thing' that removed it—namely, the Roman people that destroyed the Temple—will be laid waste, there will be 1,290 years. The *days* mentioned here are years, as in the expression, *'yamim' shall he have the right of redemption,*[95] [*yamim,* literally means 'days' but connotes 'a full year']. Likewise, *'miyamim yamimah'*[96] [literally means 'from day to day,' but here it signifies 'from year to year']. Similarly, [in the expression], *'yamim' or ten,*[97] [the word *yamim* literally means 'days,' but here it is used in the sense of 'a year']. Afterwards, Daniel said, *Happy is he that waiteth, and cometh to the thousand three hundred and five and thirty days.*[98] He thus added forty-five years to [the original 1,290 years]. The purport thereof is as follows: At the first designated time [1,290] the Messiah will come and annihilate the *detestable thing* which worships that which is no god and obliterate it from the world. He will then gather the banished ones of Israel *into the wilderness of the peoples,*[99] as it is said, *and I will bring her into the wilderness, and speak tenderly unto her,*[100] and Israel will come into their Land. [The Messiah's activities will thus] parallel what Moses our teacher, peace be upon him, the first redeemer, did. These things will transpire for forty-five years, after which Israel will rest upon their Land and will rejoice *with the Eternal their G-d, and David their king.*[101] Happy is he who waits [and reaches] those good days. Since the time of the destruction, we have now [endured] 1,195 years.[102] Thus, [we] are ninety-five years short of the count [of 1,290] that Daniel mentioned, and we hope that the redeemer will come at that time. This explanation is correct and fitting, and it is reasonable to believe in it."[103]

(94) This is probably because he will set the time of the final redemption for the year 1358 Common Era, some ninety-five years later. (95) Leviticus 25:29. (96) Exodus 13:10. (97) Genesis 24:55. (98) Daniel 12:12. (99) Ezekiel 20:35. (100) Hosea 2:16. (101) Jeremiah 30:9. (102) From the destruction of the Temple in 3828 until the disputation in 5023, there were 1,195 years. (103) In the Fourth Gate of the Book of Redemption,

62 Fray Pul rejoined, "The Sages said in the Hagadah:[104] 'What are these extra [forty-five] days [added by Daniel to the 1,290 he originally mentioned, thus making the total 1,335]? These are the forty-five days during which the redeemer will be hidden from them. Just as Moses, the first redeemer, was revealed and hidden[105] from them, so the final redeemer will reveal himself and be hidden from them.' Since the Rabbis specified [the term] 'day,' they meant actual days and not years."

63 I explained, "The Midrash chose the language of the verse [*Happy is he that waiteth . . . 'days'*][98] and it mentioned 'forty-five days' which represent years, as the Rabbis say,[106] 'The Sage quoted the language of Scripture.' "

64 Fray Pul argued that there is no Jew in the world who will not admit that the term *yom* means really a day.

65 He shouted [his objection] to the king, and they led in the first Jew they found and asked him, "What does the word *yom* in your language mean?" He answered, "*Dia* (day)."

66 I said, "My lord king, this Jew is fit to sit in judgment on Fray Pul but not on me. In Scriptural language *yom* refers to time, such as, *on the 'day' that I smote all the firstborn.*[107] In the aggregate, it is used to express years,[108] and here [in the Book of Daniel], Scripture uses it to express years. This was because he wanted to seal the matter [of the

Ramban elaborates, "We are not prophets to declare [the end] by [revealing] the secrets of G-d. Rather, we hope for the [designated] time that [the Messiah] will come . . . " (104) Yalkut Hoshea 518. (105) See Ramban, Exodus, p. 62, that Moses after his first appearance to the children of Israel in Egypt, he was then hidden from them for a certain period of time. (106) Baba Metzia 2a. Our editions of the Gemara read "the language of the world." (107) Numbers 3:17. Since the firstborn were smitten at nighttime, the word *yom* (day) must connote time, not actually day. (108) Judges 17:10: *and I will give thee ten pieces of silver 'l'yamim'* (by the year).

end of the exile], as the angel told [Daniel] several times, *Shut up the words, and seal the book, even to the time of the end; many shall run to and fro, and knowledge shall be increased.*[109] However, I speak words of wisdom with [Fray Pul], who neither knows nor understands, and it would be appropriate that he be judged by fools.

67 Fray Arnaldo de Segurra[110] offered, "Note that [in his Latin translation of the Bible], Jerome interpreted the word *yamim* here as [referring to] the ages of the people."

68 I rejoiced at his words and said, "From [Jerome's] words, you can see that the word *yamim* here is not to be taken literally as it is in the other places. Thus, he [Jerome] required the interpretation. Nevertheless, I am of the opinion that what [Jerome] called 'the ages of the people' are [actually] years, for people say, 'Many days have passed since a certain event,' and [the expression] refers to many years."

69 [Fray Pul] reverted [to his questioning] and said, "Behold, their Sages say[111] That Messiah entered the Garden of Eden [alive]. There in the Hagadah it is stated, 'Why did Messiah [enter the Garden of Eden]? It is because he saw his ancestors worshipping idols, and he separated himself from their way and served the Holy One, blessed be He, and He reserved him for the Garden of Eden.' "

70 I derided him, saying, "This serves as proof for me that [he] the descendant of idolatrous parents, was but a real man, and the Holy One, blessed be He, favorably repaid him when he separated himself from the ways of his ancestors and did not worship the idols as they did. Can this be said of G-d Himself?" I then took his book and recited the text for them from the beginning. It states that there were

(109) Daniel 12:4. (110) A Dominican scholar. (111) Derech Eretz Zuta, end of Chapter 1.

fourteen[112] who entered the Garden of Eden alive, including Serach daughter of Asher and Bathyah daughter of Pharaoh.[113] If the Nazarene were G-d, as you believe he would not be among the women in the Garden of Eden! The heaven [should be] his throne, and the earth [should be] his footstool[114]—far be it! It is instead as I say: [115] [The Messiah, a mortal] stays in the Garden of Eden, in the house of the first man before he sinned. This is the opinion of the Sages in the books of Hagadah.[116]

71 Our lord king then arose, and [he and all his entourage] left.

72 Afterwards, on the fifth day[117] [of the week], our lord the king set his royal palace as the place where the debate was to be held, saying it should be held without ostentation. We sat near the entrance to the palace. Fray Pul opened with meaningless words of no interest. Afterwards, he declared, "I will bring proof from their great sage, who has been unparalleled in his greatness for the past four hundred years. His name is Moses [Maimonides] of Egypt, and he states that the Messiah will die and his son and grandson will rule after him, and not, as you have said, that he will not die as other people do." He asked for the Book of Shoftim.[118]

(112) In our editions of Derech Eretz Zuta, only nine are enumerated. In Aleph Beth of Ben Sira (Eisenstein's, Otzar Midrashim, p. 50), eleven are listed, but Messiah is not among them. (113) At the moment of Israel's departure from Egypt, Serach was instrumental in locating the coffin which contained the remains of Joseph (Sotah 13a). Bathyah was deserving her reward for saving the life of the infant Moses. (114) See Isaiah 66:1. (115) See Paragraph 40. (116) Another version: "in this book of Hagadah," that is, the volume from which he was reading. (117) Thursday, July 26, 1263.—Another version reads: "On the third day," meaning the third day of the disputation. (118) The last of the fourteen books of Maimonides' Mishneh Torah is named Shoftim or Judges. There at the end, he speaks of the Messiah.

73 I said before them, "It is not found thus in that book. However, I admit that there are some of our Sages who say, as I mentioned earlier,[119] that in the opinion of the books of Hagadah, he was born on the day of the destruction [of the Temple] and lives forever. Yet, the opinion of the masters of the literal meaning is that he will be born close to the time of the designated period of the redemption. He will live normally for many years and die in honor, and he will bequeath his crown to his son. I have already stated that I believe in this view and that the only difference between the present world and the era of the Messiah is political subjection."

74 At this time, they brought the text which [Fray Pul] had requested, and he searched [for the passage in question] but could not find it. I then took the book from his hand and said, "Hear the words of the book which he brings," and I recited to them from the beginning of the chapter:[120] "King Messiah is destined to arise for Israel, and he will build the Temple and gather the banished of Israel."

75 Fray Arnaldo de Segurra[110] declared, "He [Maimonides] utters lies!"

76 I retorted, "Until now, he was the greatest sage, and now he is a liar!"

77 The king rebuked [Fray Arnaldo], "It is not proper to show disrespect to scholars."

78 I said to the king, "[Maimonides] is not lying, for I will prove from the Torah and from the prophets that all that he stated is true.

(119) In Paragraph 39. (120) Hilchoth Melachim 12:1.

Upon the Messiah will fall the task of gathering the banished of Israel and the dispersed ones of Judah—twelve tribes—but the Nazarene gathered no one. He did not live during the time of the exile [and had no occasion to redeem them]. The Messiah will have to build the Temple in Jerusalem, but the Nazarene neither built [the Temple] nor destroyed it. The Messiah will rule over all peoples, but [the Nazarene] did not even rule over himself." [That is, he had not sufficient dominion to prevent his persecution and execution.] Then I read them the passage [in the Torah] which begins, *And it shall come to pass, when all these things are come upon thee, the blessing and the curse, which I have set before thee,*[121] and concluded the passage until [the words], *And the Eternal thy G-d will put all these curses upon thine enemies, and on them that hate thee, that persecuted thee.*[122] I explained to them that *thine enemies* are the Christians, and they *that hate thee* are the Arabs, the two nations which persecute us. They did not answer at all, and they left.

79 On the next day, the sixth day [of the week],[123] they arranged to have the session held in the palace. *And the king sat upon his seat, as at other times, even upon the seat by the wall.*[124] Present were the bishop [of Barcelona] and many princes, Guilles de Sargon, Pere Bargo, numerous knights, many townsfolk, and the poorest of the people.

80 I said to the king, "I do not wish to continue the discussion."

81 "Why?" asked the king.

82 I explained, "There is a throng of [Jewish] people here, and all of them have urged me and begged me to discontinue [the debate], for

(121) Deuteronomy 30:1. (122) *Ibid.*, Verse 7. (123) Another version: "On the fourth day," that is, the fourth session. (124) I Samuel 20:25.

they are very much afraid of these people, the preachers who terrorize the world. The great priests and noblemen also sent me word that I should not continue this any further. Many knights of your royal household, my lord king, told me that I act unwisely by speaking in their presence against their faith. Fray Pere of Genoa, the Franciscan scholar told me that the discussion does not proceed well. The townspeople likewise remarked to some of the Jews that I should not continue." Indeed, that was so, but when they perceived [that it was] the king's will [to continue the discussion], they hesitatingly said that I should proceed. The exchange among us on this question was prolonged. Finally, I said that I would continue the disputation but that justice demands that for one day, I ask [some questions] and Fray Pul answer me, since he had been asking me [questions] and I had been answering him for three days.

83 The king decided, "Nevertheless, you will answer [his questions]." I agreed.

84 [Fray Pul] then arose and asked, "Do you believe that the Messiah of whom the prophets spoke will be an actual man or a real G-d?"

85 I replied, "Originally, we made a condition that at the beginning, we would speak of whether the Messiah had already come and that afterwards, we would discuss whether he is G-d Himself. Since you have not established that he came—for I have refuted all of the foolish proofs that you have brought—I am now vindicated in this encounter, for [the burden of] bringing proof is upon you. You accepted this condition upon yourself. If you will not admit that I have been vindicated, I will take it upon myself to bring real proofs [to convince you], if you will hear me. After it will have been explained that your Nazarene was not the Messiah, there will be no point in your discussing if the Messiah who is destined to come to us will be truly mortal or, [if not], what he will be."

86 The scholarly judges who were present said that justice is with me concerning this [point].

87 The king, however, instructed me, "Answer [his question] nevertheless."

88 I said, "In truth, the Messiah who will come will really be man, a son born out of the union of a man and a woman, even as I am. He will be of the lineage of David and his descendants, as it is written, *And there shall come forth a shoot out of the stock of Jesse,* etc.[125] It is further stated, *until 'Shiloh' cometh.*[126] [*Shiloh*] means 'his son,' [that is, a son of the tribe of Judah. The term is] related to the expression *shilyah* (afterbirth),[127] for as all other people, he will be born in an afterbirth. If he were the Spirit of G-d, as you assert, he would not be *of the stock of Jesse,* and even if he did tarry in the womb of a woman who is of [Jesse's] stock, he would not inherit the kingdom, for by law of the Torah, daughters and their seed do not inherit when there is a male [descendant],[128] and David always had male descendants."

89 [Fray Pul] said, "The psalm states, *A psalm of David. The Eternal saith unto my lord, Sit thou at My right hand.*[129] Whom, other than G-d [Himself], would King David call *my lord,* and [if you insist that David is indeed referring to a man and not G-d], how can a man sit at the right hand of G-d?"[130]

90 The king commented, He asks well, for if the Messiah were really a man of the actual seed of David, David would not address him

(125) Isaiah 11:1. (126) Genesis 49:10. (127) This interpretation of *Shiloh* is found in Midrash Lekach Tov. (128) Baba Bathra 115b. (129) Psalms 110:1. (130) In other words, since it could not be said of a human being that he sits at G-d's right hand, the verse must refer to the Messiah, who Fray Pul contends, is a divinity.

as *my lord*. If I had a son or grandson of my seed, I would not refer to him as 'my lord' even if he were to have dominion over the whole world. Rather, I would want him to call me 'my lord,' and [I would desire] that he should kiss my hand."

91 I turned my face to Fray Pul and said [rebukingly], "Are you the Jewish scholar who discovered this argument and who was so moved by it as to become converted? Is it you who advises the king to gather the Jewish scholars to yourself [so that you can] dispute with them about these new finds that you have discovered? Have we not heard this before? Why, there is not a priest or a child who does not ask this question of the Jews. This question is very old."

92 The king directed "Nevertheless, answer it."

93 I said, "Hear me now. King David was the composer who wrote the Psalms with [the aid of] the Holy Spirit. He composed them for the purpose of having them sung before the altar of G-d. He himself did not sing them, nor was he permitted to do so, for that [function] was forbidden to him by law of the Torah.[131] Instead, he gave the Psalms to the Levites [so that they would] sing them. This is clearly written in [the Book of] Chronicles.[132] Therefore, [King David] perforce expressed the psalm in the language appropriate for utterance by the Levite. Thus, if [King David] had said, 'the Eternal said to me,' the Levite [repeating these words] would be uttering falsehood. Instead, it is proper for the Levite to say in the Temple, *The Eternal saith unto my lord*—[that is], to David—*Sit thou at My right hand.* The purport of the [term] 'sitting' is to state that the Creator, blessed be He, will protect him during his lifetime and that He will save him and cause him to prevail over his enemies. So it was, *for he lifted up his spear against eight hundred, whom he slew at one time.*[133] Can any one

(131) Deuteronomy 18:7. See "The Commandments," Vol. I, pp. 32-33. (132) I Chronicles 16:7. (133) II Samuel 23:8.

among these knights before you do so in his prowess? This is the *right hand* of G-d [mentioned in the psalm: *Sit thou at My right hand*]. It is also written of David, *And thy right hand hath holden me up.*[134] [It is] similarly [written], *The right hand of the Eternal doeth valiantly. The right hand of the Eternal is exalted.*[135] Regarding Moses our teacher, peace be upon him, it is written, *He caused His glorious arm to go at the right hand of Moses,*[136] and [Moses] said at the fall of Pharaoh, *Thy right hand, O Eternal, dasheth in pieces the enemy.*[137] Moreover, in [various] places, the Scriptural verses mention [the proper noun instead of the pronoun]: *and Jephthah and Samuel;*[138] *ye wives of Lemech.*[139] All the words of Moses our teacher in the Torah are in a similar vein.[140] Here, however, he had to express it as I have mentioned.[141] The Psalms were written with [the aid of] the Holy Spirit and were said with reference to David and his son who sits on his throne. This is the Messiah, for just as events were partially [favorable] to David, so will they be generally [favorable] to Messiah his son. *The right hand* of the Holy One, blessed be He, which supported David until he prevailed over his enemies round about him will also support the Messiah until he will make all the nations his footstool. They are all his enemies, for they subjected his people and denied his coming and his kingdom. Some of them [even] made [themselves] another such claimant. Thus, it is proper to chant this psalm in the Temple in the days of David and in the days of the Messiah his son, for it is composed with reference *to the throne of David and to his kingdom.*"[142]

(134) Psalms 18:36. (135) *Ibid.*, 118:15-16. (136) Isaiah 63:12. (137) Exodus 15:6. (138) I Samuel 12:1. In this case, Samuel was saying that G-d had sent various leaders to help Israel, but since he himself was the speaker, he should have said, "and Jephtah and me."—Here too, in the case of the verse in question from Psalms it should have said, "G-d said to me," but it is the Scriptural style to use the proper name or title. Hence, "*The Eternal saith unto 'my lord.'*" (139) Genesis 4:23. Lemech was the speaker, and he should have said, "My wives." (140) See Ramban, Deuteronomy, Introduction. (141) Had David said, "G-d said to me," the Levite singing the psalm would have been uttering falsehood, since G-d had not spoken to that Levite. (142) Isaiah 9:6.

94 Fray Pul objected, "How could he say this thing? Their Sages state that [this psalm] speaks of the Messiah, that the words are meant literally, and that he sits to *the right hand* of G-d?" He cited a Hagadah which says, "In the future, the Holy One, blessed be He, will seat Messiah to His right hand and Abraham to His left."

95 I replied, "This [Hagadah] also proves my point, for I have already stated that the intent thereof partly concerns David and that its main feature deals completely with the Messiah." I asked for the book, and he gave it to me.

96 I continued, "See how fraudulent he is! This Hagadah states: In the future, the Holy One, blessed be He, will seat Messiah to His right hand and Abraham to His left. Abraham's face became grieved, and he said, 'A descendant of mine sits to the right hand of the Holy One, blessed be He, and I to His left!' The Holy One, blessed be He, then appeased him, etc.[143] It is clear [from here] that Messiah is not G-d, and that the Nazarene is not the Messiah at all. If he were G-d, Abraham would not have been jealous if G-d were accorded more honor, and his face would not at all have become pale and crestfallen. Abraham called [Messiah] *'ben b'ni,'* (a son of my son), – [that is, 'a descendant of mine'], not *ben biti* (a son of my daughter). According to your words, [though], the Nazarene is not at all a male descendant of Abraham. Further, Messiah's sitting to the right [of G-d] is like Abraham's sitting to the left,[144] both being real men. It is also obvious that the Nazarene is not Messiah, for [the Midrash] speaks of 'the future,' and these Sages [of the Midrash] who stated it lived about five hundred years after [the Nazarene]. However, Fray Pul consumes [only] the beginning and end [of the passage] and feels no shame [for having omitted the context]."

(143) G-d appeased Abraham by saying, "Your descendant will sit at your right hand, and I will be at your right." (144) In other words, the Midrash indicates that the same activity of sitting is involved equally in the case of both Abraham and Messiah, for both are on a similar level.

97 Again he reverted [to his line of argument] and cited proof from the Midrash[145] in which they say: "It is written, *And I will walk among you.*[146] They devised a parable. This can be compared to a king who went out to walk leisurely with his laborer in his orchard, but the laborer avoided him. The king asked him, 'Why do you hide? I am as you are.' In the same manner, the Holy One, blessed be He, will walk leisurely with the righteous in the Garden of Eden. However, when the righteous will see Him, they will be frightened before Him. The Holy One, blessed be He, will say to the righteous, Why are you afraid of Me? I am as you are. I might think that My fear will not be upon you. Scripture therefore states, *and I will be your G-d, and ye shall be My people.*"[146] Now, [Fray Pul concluded], 'Since [G-d] said, 'I am as you are,' it shows that He turned [into a] man as they were."

98 I rejoined, "All that he cited—[if he would understand it]—is proof against him. This episode refers to the future and will occur in the Garden of Eden. The Nazarene, however, did not walk leisurely with the righteous in the Garden of Eden when he was still alive. Instead, he was a fugitive from his enemies and pursuers all through his lifetime. This Midrash, though, is a parable, just as it begins: 'They devised a parable: This can be compared, etc.' The purport thereof is that the righteous in this world cannot conceive the truth of [the nature of] prophecy and they cannot see that which is called the [Divine] Glory, as He said, *In a vision do I make Myself known unto him.*[147] At the beginning of his [state of] prophecy, even Moses our teacher was frightened, as it is said, *And Moses hid his face, for he was afraid,* etc.[148] In the future, however, their souls will be cleansed of all sin and pernicious matter, and they will be permitted to contemplate [the Divine Glory] through a lucid speculum as did Moses our teacher, peace be upon him, of whom Scripture said, *And the Eternal spoke unto Moses face to face, as a man speaketh to his friend,* etc.[149] That

(145) Yalkut *Bechukothai* 672, with minor changes. (146) Leviticus 26:12. (147) Numbers 12:6. (148) Exodus 3:6. (149) *Ibid.*, 33:11.

[statement of the Rabbis in the Midrash], 'I am as you are,' was [expressed] by way of comparison so that the righteous should not be frightened and fearful [in G-d's presence] just as they are not afraid of one another. This is the intent of the Scriptural expression, *as a man speaketh to his friend,*[149] for G-d did not turn [into a] man when he was speaking with Moses. It is the language of the Sages. This is analogous to their statement in Yelamdeinu: [150] 'If you perform My commandments, you are as I am.' It is also the Scriptural style, [as in this verse], *And ye shall be as G-d, knowing [good and evil],*[151] and [in the verses]: *Behold, the man is become as one of us;*[152] *and he that stumbleth among them at that day shall be as David, and the House of David shall be like angels.*[153] However, [it was] not [intended to suggest] that they are equal "in their similarity."

99 [Fray Pul] reverted [to his contention] and argued, "In Bereshith Rabbah, they say,[154] '*And the spirit of G-d hovered over the face of the waters.*[155] This is the spirit of Messiah.' If so, [Messiah] is not man; he is the spirit of G-d."

100 I replied, "Woe to him who knows nothing and thinks that he is wise and erudite. [The Rabbis] further state there, '*And the spirit of G-d hovered.*[155] This is the spirit of the first man.' Did they say that he will be G-d? He who does not know what is above and what is below in books, now perverts the words of the living G-d! However, the lecturer who interpreted [the above verse to mean that] 'this is the spirit of Messiah' explained the verse as referring to the [four] kingdoms [of the world]. He interpreted the language of the verse here as a reference to future events. Thus he said: '*And the earth was 'tohu' (unformed).*[155] This is Babylon, as it is said, *I beheld the earth, and lo, it was 'tohu' (waste).*[156] *And void.*[155] This is Media, as it is said, *And*

(150) I do not know its source. (151) Genesis 3:5. (152) *Ibid.*, Verse 22. (153) Zechariah 12:8. (154) Bereshith Rabbah 2:5. (155) Genesis 1:2. (156) Jeremiah 4:23. The prophet was referring to the destruction that

they hastened to bring Haman.[157] *And darkness.*[155] This is Greece, which darkened the eyes of Israel with decrees [against their religion]. *Over the face of the deep.*[155] This is the wicked kingdom [of Rome]. *And the spirit of G-d.*[155] This is the spirit of Messiah. By what merit [will it come? It will come by the merit indicated in the phrase] *hovering over the face of the waters,*[155] [that is] by merit of repentance, which is compared to water.'[158] Thus, the Midrash records the four kingdoms, including the fourth kingdom, which is Rome. Afterwards, it introduces *the spirit of G-d* that represents the Messiah, a real man, full of wisdom and full of the spirit of G-d, as were Bezalel, of whom it is said, *and I have filled him with the spirit of G-d,* etc.[159] – and Joshua – of whom it was said, *And Joshua the son of Nun was full of the spirit of wisdom.*[160] It now stands explained that [in the above Midrash], they were speaking of the Messiah who is destined to come after the fourth kingdom." I was unable to tell him the purport of the Midrash, for it is based upon intimations, which [the Rabbis] interpret on the strength of linguistic allusions. [The intent], though, is not that this is the essential [meaning of] Scripture in this place. Similar instances are found in most places throughout Bereshith Rabbah, just as they say in [the section of] *Vayeitzei Yaakov.*[161] I said this in order to show all of them that [Fray Pul] did not know how to read the book he brought, for he erred in the reading of the language.

101 The king then arose, and they all followed.

Babylon would wreak upon the kingdom of Judah. (157) Esther 6:14. The Hebrew words *vavohu* (and void) and *vayavhilu* (and they hastened) are etymologically related (Matnoth Kehunah). (158) As it says, *pour out thy heart like water* (Lamentations 2:19). (159) Exodus 31:3. (160) Deuteronomy 34:9. (161) Genesis 28:10. The Midrash there interprets Jacob's dream of the ladder and the angels ascending and descending upon it as references to the four kingdoms which will appear in the history of the world and affect Israel. See Ramban Genesis, pp. 349-350.

102 This is an account of all the discussions. To my knowledge, I have not altered anything in it. After this [final session] on the same day, I stood before our lord king, and he said, "Let the disputation remain [as it is], for I have never seen a man who is not right[162] argue his case as well," [that is], as [well as] I have done. I then heard in the court that it is the wish of the king and the preachers to come to the synagogue on the day of the Sabbath. I therefore remained in the city [of Barcelona] eight days. When they came [to the synagogue on] the following Sabbath,[163] I answered our lord king fittingly [and] properly, for he lectured vigorously that the Nazarene was the deliverer.

103 I arose and said, "The words of our lord king delivered before princes and distinguished nobles—coming, as they do, from the mouth of an exalted and honored prince—are unique in the world, but I will not praise them [by saying] that they are true, for I have clear proofs and texts as bright as the sun that the truth is not as he said. However, he [the speaker—that is, Ramban himself] is not worthy [enough] to dispute with him. Yet, I will say one thing about which I am very much amazed at him. The things he said in our presence to make us believe that the Nazarene is the deliverer [were said by] the Nazarene himself [when he] brought the same message to our ancestors and tried to tell it to them. They refuted him to his face with a perfect and strong rejection [despite the fact that] it was he [himself speaking], who knew and could argue his claim that he was G-d, in accordance with your opinion, better than the king [can today]. Now, if our ancestors who saw him and knew him did not heed him, how can we believe and heed the voice of the king, whose only knowledge of the matter stems merely [from the hearsay] of distant reporters who heard it from people who neither knew him nor were his countrymen as our ancestors knew [him] and were witnesses [to his life]!

(162) Another version: "who is not legally trained." (163) This was the twenty-sixth of Ab (August 4, 1263). It was *Parshath R'eih* (see Introduction).

104 Afterwards, Fray Ramon de Penyafort[17] arose and lectured on the trinity, saying that it is wisdom, will, and power. He declared in the synagogue, "The Master [Ramban] agreed to this in Gerona; [he concurred] with the words of Fray Pul."

105 I stood up and objected, "Hearken and hear my words, Jews and gentiles. Fray Pul asked me in Gerona if I believe in the trinity. I asked him, 'What is the trinity? [Does it mean] that G-d is [composed of] three coarse bodies like [the bodies], of men?' He answered, 'No.' [I asked], 'Are they three ethereal substances like souls or three angels?' He said, 'No.' [I inquired further], 'Is it one thing composed of three [elements] as [physical] bodies consist of the four elements?' He said, 'No.' If so, [I challenged], 'What is the trinity?' He answered, '[It is] the wisdom, will, and power.' I said, 'I admit that G-d is wise and not foolish, that He has will without emotion, and that He is powerful and not weak. However, the expression trinity is a fundamental error, for wisdom is not [an external element of] chance in the Creator. Rather, He and His Wisdom are One, He and His Will are One, He and His Power are One, if so, wisdom, will, and power are all One. Even if He were affected by [external] chances, that which is G-dly would still not be three, but G-d, He is the One Who is the Subject of the three [elements of] chance.' At this point, our lord king expressed an analogy which the deceivers taught him. He said that there are three things in wine—color, taste, and smell—and [yet] they are one. However, this is a fundamental error, for the color, taste, and smell in the wine are separate things. Each can be found without the other, for there are red and white and other colored [wines]. The same applies to taste and smell. Moreover, the wine is not the redness or the taste or the smell; it is the substance of the wine [itself] that fills the vessels. Thus, [the wine] is a substance carrying three different properties in which there is no unity. Should we mistakenly [count the Divine Wisdom, Will, and Power as three separate entities], then perforce we should be [properly] speaking of a unit of four [components, for the Being Who is G-d and His Wisdom, Will, and Power should [all] be counted, which make four. Moreover, you should be speaking of five,

for He is living, and life in Him is [as essential] as wisdom, and He would be then defined as living, wise, willing, powerful, and the essence of G-dliness, [all of] which are five! However, all this is a clear mistake."

106 Fray Pul then arose and declared that he believes in the real unity and that nevertheless they are three. [He said] further that it is a very profound matter which [even] the angels and the ministers on high do not understand.

107 I arose and said, "It is clear that man does not believe what he does not know. If so, the angels [too] cannot believe in the trinity." His friends prevented [Fray Pul] from answering [further].

108 The king then stood and descended from the pulpit, and they left [the synagogue]. On the following day, I stood before our lord king, and he said to me, "Return to your city, to life, and to peace." He gave me three hundred *dinarim*.[164] I parted from him in abounding love.[165] May G-d make me worthy of life in the World to Come. Amen.

(164) A document recounting this episode exists. It contains the king's admission of the debt he owes a Jewish merchant of Barcelona, whom he had ordered to give three hundred *dinarim* to "the Rabbi of Gerona." Y. Baer, A History of the Jews in Christian Spain, J.P.S., 1966, Vol. I, pp. 153-154, relates that the coins were *solidi*. The original document is found in J. Regnee, Catalogue des Actes de Jaime Ier . . . concernant les Juifs, § 319. (165) The respect was no doubt mutual, as is evident from the ensuing events in which the king defended Ramban in the action taken against him by the Dominicans (see Introduction to the Discourse on Koheleth).

Recommended Readings

- Torah: The Five Books of Moses - The Interlinear Bible: Hebrew / English
- The Psalms: Hebrew Text & English Translation - Parallel Bible: Hebrew/English
- Wealth: A Torah Approach
- The General Theory of Employment, Interest, and Money by John Maynard Keynes
- The Bible as History in Pictures by Werner Keller
- Kabbalah and the Age of the Universe by Aryeh Kaplan
- Pray and Grow Rich by Catherine Ponder

Lightning Source UK Ltd.
Milton Keynes UK
UKHW010816300822
408024UK00002B/373

9 781684 114009